Something Even Better Is Coming

by

Sharyn Ferrie

Something
Even Better
Is Coming

 O ne warm, summer afternoon, seven-year-old Maya and her grandma strolled hand in hand along a path in the wooded area of a park.

They chatted about this and that.

They listened to the birds singing joyfully and were delighted at the antics of the squirrels as they ran up and down the trees and jumped from branch to branch.

Maya and her grandma enjoyed spending time together.

At the base of a tall oak tree, they discovered a bird's nest that had fallen to the ground.

Maya picked up a stick and poked the nest and discovered three broken eggs inside, but the baby birds had died.

She said, "Grandma, this makes me sad. I hate when anything dies."

Grandma admired Maya's compassionate heart.

She answered, "Maya, it hurts when pets or people we love have to leave us. But God knows the length of each life including animals, flowers, trees and even people."

Ecclesiastes 3:1, Psalm 139:1-24

Maya nodded her head and replied, "When my cat died, I cried for a long time."

Grandma placed her arm on Maya's shoulder as they continued walking along the path, then replied,

"I remember, honey. I think God gave us pets to show us His perfect love. When they leave us, that hurts our heart, but God brings another pet to continue to show us His love."

"Yes, that's what happened," Maya replied. "Our new cat, Socks, is a lot of fun, and I love him too."

They continued talking as they followed the path out of the wooded area. As the playground came into sight, Maya stopped walking and looked up at her grandma.

"I was just thinking, Grandma. There's only one of you. You can't be replaced! One day, you'll get old and die."

Grandma sat on a park bench and put her arm around Maya. She gazed into her granddaughter's soft, brown eyes, shining with tears, then drew Maya close for a grandma-hug and whispered, "I'm not afraid of dying, honey."

God promised that by accepting His gift of forgiveness when Jesus died for us, we would have eternal life.

"Do you know what that means?"

Maya nodded her head.

"Well, I know that Jesus is God. He became a man, lived a sinless life, and died for our sins on the cross. But what is eternal life? "

Grandma smiled. "Eternal means forever."

"God promises that everyone who believes that Jesus died for their sins will have eternal life."

"Because of the power of God inside Himself, Jesus rose from the dead."

"From that point forward, death could no longer keep us from God." *II Cor. 5:21*

With tears springing to her eyes, Maya cried,

"But you're getting older and one day you'll die!"

"Where is the eternal life God promised you?"

"Maybe I can explain it to you in a way that you'll understand, honey." answered Grandma.

Patting the bench, she said, "Sit down next to me and I'll tell you a story."

Maya always enjoyed her grandma's stories.

She sat down and watched her grandma's face as she began to speak.

"Maya, before you were born, God knew you."

"He mixed a bit of your mother and a bit of your father together and a little something special that was all you and then God placed you in your mommy's womb." *Psalm 139:16*

"Teeny, tiny, little you enjoyed being able to swim around, do somersaults, kicks off the sides and even clap your hands."

Maya laughed and said, "It sounds like I was in a large swimming pool."

"That's right, it does" chuckled Grandma.

"You liked it there, Maya."

"You were fed and kept warm, and you thought, 'This is a fine place to be.'"

"Then you heard a soft voice whisper, **'Soon, I'll have something even better for you.'"**

"But you thought, I like it here just fine. I'm staying right here."

Maya laughed again and asked, "Was that God whispering to me?"

Grandma smiled and answered, "Yes, sweetheart. God's always been near you."

Grandma continued, "Over the next couple of months, you went through changes in your body. You developed fingers and toes and little ears and a nose. Your heart was beating stronger every day."

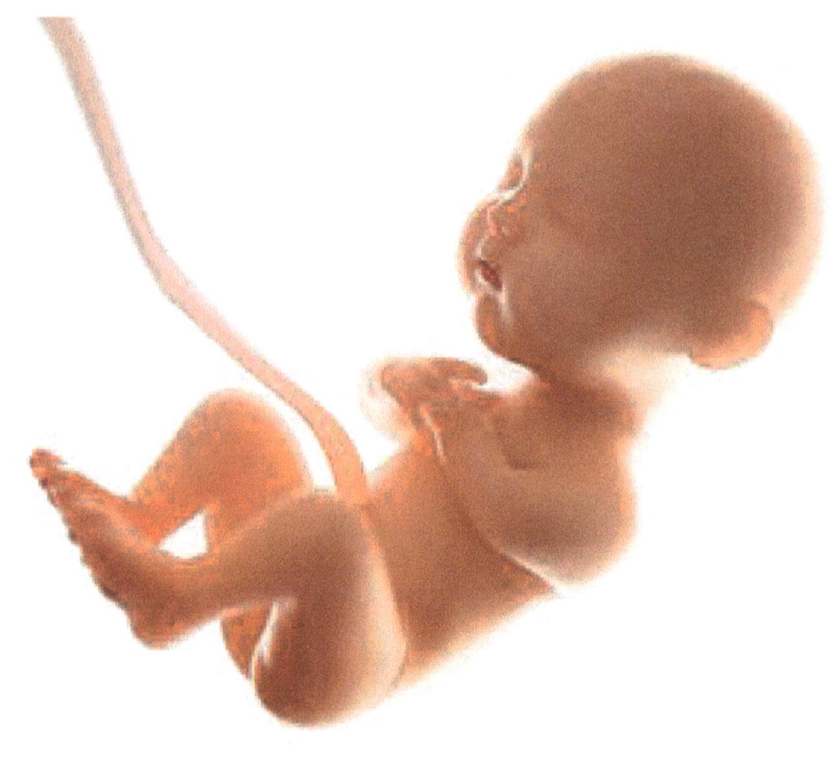

Maya asked, "Could I see, hear or smell anything?"

"No, before you were born, you couldn't see, hear or smell anything, but you could feel what you touched," answered Grandma.

"It was dark inside your mommy, but you weren't afraid. Not at all!"

"You had fun every day, moving back and forth, kicking off the sides of the walls, clapping your hands, playing with your fingers and toes and punching the sides of the wall."

Maya laughed. "Maybe that's why I'm such a good kicker when I play soccer."

Grandma laughed. "That might be why. You had a lot of practice even before you were born."

"Then you heard that soft voice whisper again, **'Soon, I'll have something even better for you.'**"

"But you thought, 'Nope, I'm staying right here'."

"A couple of months later, it was starting to get cramped inside your mommy."

"You were growing bigger and couldn't move around as easily."

"You couldn't do somersaults at all."

"You could still kick and punch the walls, but it was harder to clap your hands."

"Then that soft voice whispered,

'It's almost time, little one.

I have something even better for you.'"

"Again, you thought, 'No! I'm staying right here!' You kicked your mommy extra hard just to prove your point."

Maya giggled and said, "Mommy was probably getting tired of me punching and kicking her."

"Yes, I think she was," Grandma laughed.

"Then one day, you discovered that you were upside down and you felt a force pushing on you. You didn't like that at all."

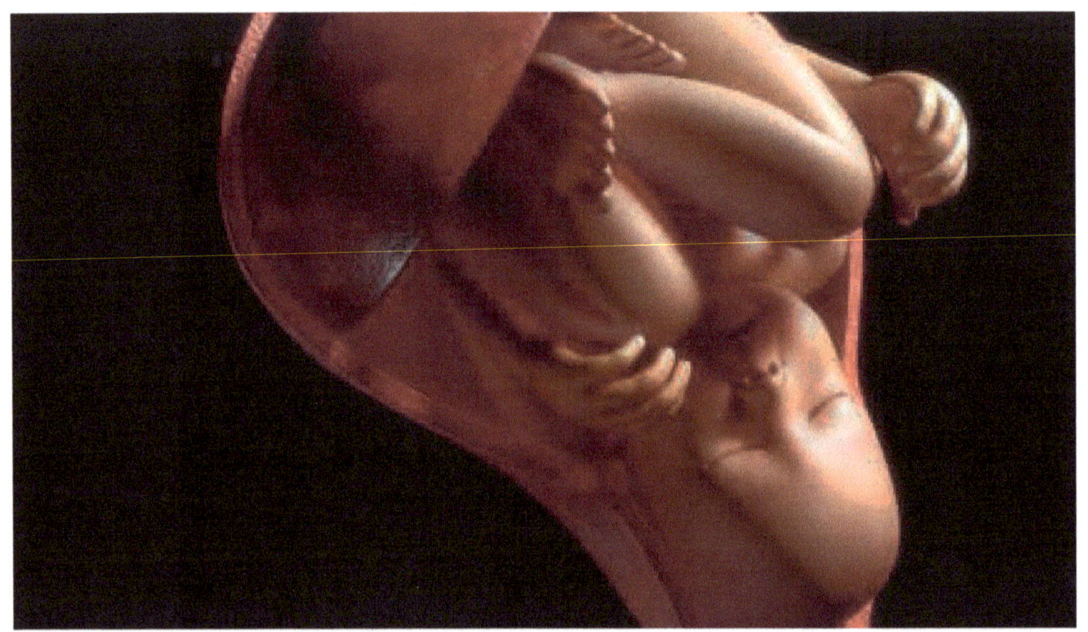

"That soft gentle voice whispered,

'Today's the day, precious one."

"I have something much better for you.'"

"As loudly as you could, you yelled out,

'Noooooooooooo!'"

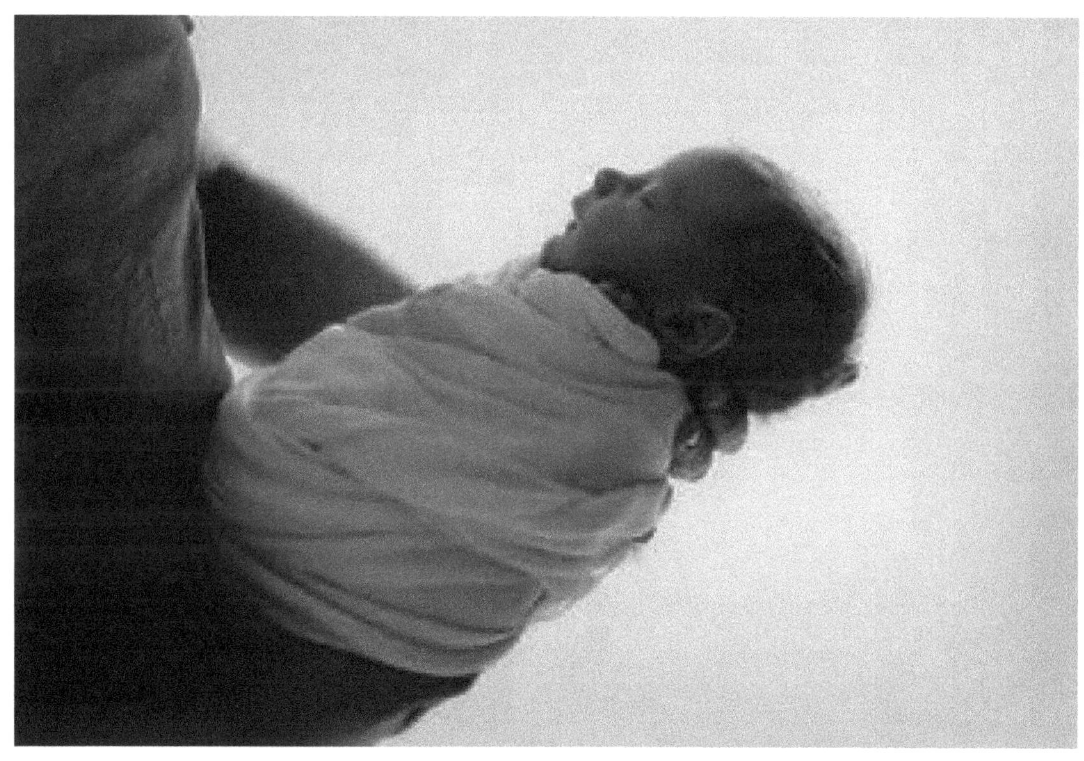

"Suddenly, a pair of warm hands were holding you."

Grandma smiled as she continued, "You opened your eyes a crack and became aware of a bright light and people around you and you heard excited voices."

"They laid you on your mommy and you stared at her kind face and sweet smile and your ears heard her whisper,

"Hello Maya. I'm Mommy. I'm so happy you're here!'"

Maya smiled at hearing that.

"You were amazed and kept looking around," Grandma gave a laugh.

"You were wrapped in a warm blanket and placed in your mommy's arms, and you saw your Daddy smiling at you. You saw me, too."

"You thought, 'This is amazing. I'm going to like this place.'

That gentle voice of God whispered,

'I told you so.'"

When Grandma finished speaking, Maya's mouth hung open as she pictured in her mind what her grandma had described to her.

Then she smiled.

"Let me ask you a question, Maya," said Grandma.

"If given a choice, would you want to go back inside your mommy to live or would you want to stay here and experience what life has to offer?"

Maya laughed. "That's a silly question, Grandma. Of course, I'd want to stay here"

"Of course, you do," answered Grandma.

"Life can be so much fun, but it's more than that. This is our training ground. God allowed us to be born, hoping we'd choose to find our way back to Him."

Maya was confused and asked, "But if God is always with us, why would we have to find our way back to Him?"

Grandma smiled. "That's a good question, Maya."

"After we're born, we can still feel God around us all the time, but as we get older, we start understanding the language of those speaking to us and we start talking back to them."

"As those conversations become more frequent, we tend to stop hearing God's soft voice."

"It takes great effort to quiet our minds to listen to him talking to us."

 "Oh," Maya said, nodding. "Like when I say my prayers. God hears me and if I'm quiet, maybe I'll hear him talking back in my mind?"

"That's right, honey," answered Grandma.

"Sometimes you might have a thought come into your mind and you'll know it was from God."

"Sometimes you might feel led to do something kind for someone else. That's God speaking as well."

"For those of us who seek to know him better, he reminds us in the Bible that He loves us and has amazing plans for us in the future."

"When we rediscover God and his love for us, it's called being born again." *John 3:1-21*

*

Grandma drew Maya close to her and said, "I like to think that when it's time for me to leave this life, it will be like a graduation."

"Just like when you were born, you graduated into the life you're living now."

"God promises in the Bible that the best is yet to come in the next life to come" *1 Cor. 2:9*

"My body might get older, honey, and my mind might not always stay as sharp, but one day, I'll graduate."

"I'll experience all of the secrets things God says we can't even imagine in this life. Just like you couldn't imagine this life when you were warm inside your mommy,"

I Cor. 15:35-58

Maya's flashed her beautiful smile. "Thank you, Grandma!
I understand now!"

"Because we found God again and trust Jesus, when we die,
we leave this life and start a new life with them."

"If you go before me, I'll see you and Jesus when I get there."

"Yes, Maya." Grandma explained.

"For those of us who love him now, we'll be with him
forever- for eternity."

"But until that time, we're here to enjoy what this life has to
offer us."

"We have lessons to learn and many fascinating people to
meet."

Grandma hugged Maya.

They sat like that quietly together for a few minutes, each
lost in their own thoughts.

Slowly Grandma glanced up and looked around her.

She gave Maya another squeeze and said, "Look over by the swings, honey."

"Aren't those some of your classmates from school?"

"If you like, you can play with them while I sit here and talk to God."

Maya gave her grandma a big hug and a kiss on her cheek.

"I love you, Grandma."

"Thank you for telling me that story."

As she ran off, she called back, "Tell God I said Hi and that I love Him, too!"

"I will, little one, I surely will." Answered Grandma, as she gazed lovingly at her precious granddaughter.

Then turned her eyes upward towards Heaven and smiled.

The End is never the end.

www.ingramcontent.com/pod-product-compliance
Lightning Source LLC
Chambersburg PA
CBHW040158110726
48005CB00018B/2809